First World War
and Army of Occupation
War Diary
France, Belgium and Germany

40 DIVISION
Divisional Troops
83 Sanitary Section
7 June 1916 - 31 March 1917

WO95/2603/1

The Naval & Military Press Ltd
www.nmarchive.com
Published in association with The National Archives

Published by

The Naval & Military Press Ltd

Unit 10 Ridgewood Industrial Park,

Uckfield, East Sussex,

TN22 5QE England

Tel: +44 (0) 1825 749494

www.naval-military-press.com

www.nmarchive.com

This diary has been reprinted in facsimile from the original. Any imperfections are inevitably reproduced and the quality may fall short of modern type and cartographic standards.

© Crown Copyright
Images reproduced by permission of The National Archives, London, England, 2015.

Contents

Document type	Place/Title	Date From	Date To
Heading	WO95/2603/1 83 Sanitary Section		
Heading	40th Division 83rd Sanitary Section Jun 1916-1917 Mar To 3 Army.		
Heading	Medical Services War Diary Of 40th Divnl. (83rd) Sanitary Section month ending June 1916 July 1916 Volume I and II.		
Miscellaneous		16/08/1916	16/08/1916
Miscellaneous	Headquarters, 40th Division.	04/08/1916	04/08/1916
War Diary	Lillers	07/06/1916	15/06/1916
War Diary	Lillers to Bruay	19/06/1916	30/06/1916
War Diary	Bruay	01/07/1916	03/07/1916
War Diary	Bracquemont	04/07/1916	13/07/1916
War Diary	Bracquemont	12/07/1916	30/07/1916
Heading	40th Div. 83rd Sanitary Section. August 1916.		
War Diary	Bracquemont	01/08/1916	19/08/1916
War Diary	Les Brebis	20/08/1916	31/08/1916
Heading	40th Div. 83rd Sanitary Section. Sept. 1916.		
War Diary	Map Reference Sheet 36B France 1:40,000. 3rd Edition L35. B68.	01/09/1916	29/09/1916
Heading	40th Div. 83rd Sanitary Section. Oct. 1916.		
War Diary	L.35.B.1.9.	01/10/1916	27/10/1916
War Diary	Map Reference 36B. S.11.c.1.1.	28/10/1916	28/10/1916
War Diary	Map Reference 36B. T.9.d.2.5.	29/10/1916	31/10/1916
Heading	40th Div. 83rd Sanitary Section. Nov. 1916.		
War Diary	Lens Rocourt E2 France 100000.	01/11/1916	01/11/1916
War Diary	France Lens 100,000. Sibiville D3.	02/11/1916	03/11/1916
War Diary	France Lens 100,000 Villers Hospitals C 4.	04/11/1916	04/11/1916
War Diary	France 100,000 Lens Lanches. B5.	05/11/1916	07/11/1916
War Diary	France 100,000 Lens Bernaville B5.	08/11/1916	13/11/1916
War Diary	France Lens 100,000 C4.	15/11/1916	16/11/1916
War Diary	France Lens 100,000 E 4.	17/11/1916	17/11/1916
War Diary	France Lens 100,000 E 5.	22/11/1916	22/11/1916
War Diary	France Lens, 100000 Canaples C6	23/11/1916	23/11/1916
War Diary	France Abbeville 100000 L 6.	24/11/1916	30/11/1916
Heading	War Diary of 83rd Sanitary Section. From Dec 1st-To Dec 31st 1916 Volume VII.		
War Diary	Ailly-Le-Ht Clocher France 1/100000 Abbeville L 6.	01/12/1916	12/12/1916
War Diary	Map reference France 100,000 amiens H2b Chipilly.	15/12/1916	27/12/1916
War Diary	France 1/40000 Albert G.8.B.8.4.	28/12/1916	31/12/1916
Heading	40th Div. 83rd Sanitary Section. Jan. 1917.		
War Diary	Map Reference France 1/40,000. Albert. G8. B.8.4. Sheet 13.	01/01/1917	26/01/1917
War Diary	France 1/40000. Albert G36. d.8.3.	28/01/1917	31/01/1917
Heading	40th Div. 83rd Sanitary Section. Feb 1917.		
War Diary	Map Reference France 1/40,000 Albert g.36. d.8.3.	01/02/1917	28/02/1917
Heading	No. 83. Sanitary Section. Mar. 1917.		
War Diary	Map Reference France 1/40,000. Albert g 36 d 83.	01/03/1917	09/03/1917
War Diary	Map Albert G.8. d.1.3.	10/03/1917	22/03/1917
War Diary	Sheet 62c H.1.a.1.2.	23/03/1917	27/03/1917
War Diary	Map Reference H.7.b.9.2.	28/03/1917	31/03/1917

WO95/2603/1

83 Sanitary Section

40TH DIVISION

83RD SANITARY SECTION
JUN 1916 - ~~DEC 1916.~~
1917 MAR

TO 3 ARMY

JUNE
JULY

83 San Sec

Vol 1-2

40/

Confidential

Medical Services

War Diary

of

40th Divnl. (83rd) Sanitary Section

for month ending

June 1916

July 1916

Volumes I and II.

16.8.16.

A. J. Luther
Col.
A.D.M.S. 40th Division

COMMITTEE FOR THE
MEDICAL HISTORY OF THE WAR
Date

June & July 1916.

3

A

War Diaries Vols. I and II, for the months of June and July - of 83rd Sanitary Section - 40th Division; herewith.

A. J. Luther
Col.
A.D.M.S. 40th Division.

16.8.16.

—4—

D.A.G.,
G.H.Q.

Forwarded with reference to your No. 140/452 dated 31/7/1916.

16th August, 1916.

Major-General,
Commanding 40th Division.

Headquarters,
    40th Division.

    The War Diaries of the undermentioned Units have not been received for the months stated against them.

    It is requested that they may be forwarded as soon as possible.

    UNIT.   PERIOD.

  Ammunition Column.   June.
  83rd Sanitary Section.   June.

           (Sd.) F.C. Yates, Capt.,
General Headquarters,   for Major-General,
3rd Echelon.
31/7/1916.   D. A. C.

                  2.

~~H.Q., 40th Div. R.A.~~
A. D. M. S.

    Please issue orders for these Diaries to be despatched at once.

4th August, 1916.

                              Captain, D.A.A.&.Q.M.G.
                              40th Division.

P.T.O.

83rd SANITARY SECTION.
40th DIVISION.

Secret

Army Form C. 2118.

Instructions regarding War Diaries and Intelligence Summaries are contained in F.S. Regs., Part II and the Staff Manual respectively. Title pages will be prepared in manuscript.

WAR DIARY for JUNE. 1916.
or
INTELLIGENCE SUMMARY. VOLUME I. page 1

(Erase heading not required.)

Hour, Date, Place	Summary of Events and Information	Remarks and references to Appendices
JUNE 7. LILLERS.	Arrived from HAVRE about 1.30 a.m. Getting stores & into order. Detailing duties to men of Section. Store & mess dining place. Lt. RULE NATIONALE – Men's billet (1.N.C.O. + 23 men) CAFÉ AUX SPORTS, RUE NATIONALE. 4 N.C.O. 30 RUE NATIONALE. Officer's billet. 33. RUE NATIONALE. Field Kitchen had to be constructed on ground behind Stores & mess dining place.	
" 9.	Store-room half of which was given up to dining room & food store. Inspectors started to find the way about & learn which units had arrived in billeting area. Let me now go to test water supplies as apparently no record left by previous occupants.	
" 10.	Went over to CHOQUES to see Capt JOHNSON Sanitary officer 1st Division who gave me some particulars about district & some places of some of the Villages showing water supply &c. Lorry arrived having left Havre by road on 6th & of Corpl. GRAY. Arrangements made yesterday as to inspection of billeting areas unsatisfactory as the R.F.A. units, R.E's Divisional Cyclists &c are so far from our centre that they cannot be worked from here without Transport. Considered possibility of moving Section to a more central position of sending a sub-section to PUCHY-AU-BOIS. DADMS did not think this worth while as we were likely to move shortly.	
" 13.	The 1/4 E.H.L.I. 12/2 S.W.B & 1/2/2 Suffolks reported to A.D.M.S. for having billets, latrines &c in an insanitary condition when they moved out. Took some of my inspectors round the outlying districts in Ford Ambulance dropped them at various points to inspect. Picked them up on return. On arrival at office (usual) found orders to go to 1st Division next morning at 10 a.m. Spent evening making arrangements about the section carrying on & about getting to NOEUX-LES-MINES.	
" 14.	Received reports from inspectors as to the R.F.A. lines — which were unsatisfactory. Left Section 10 a.m. to go to 1st Division. Handed over to LIEUT. FERGUSON (135 Field Ambulance) who is to carry on during my absence, left him the reports on R.F.A. lines to deal with & told him to report on general condition of	
" 15.	things to A.D.M.S.	
" 19 LILLERS TO BRUAY.	Section left LILLERS for BRUAY. Took over 2 lorry loads of material. Marched on. Lieut FERGUSON still in charge as I am making a round of visits to the 3 Divisions of the 1st Corp.	
" 20.	Getting Stores &c into order. First billets arranged for men & the back kitchen which was to serve as Office were impossible so Lieut Ferguson saw Town Major	

83rd SANITARY SECTION.
40th DIVISION.

Secret

WAR DIARY for JUNE 1916 (continued).
INTELLIGENCE SUMMARY.
(Erase heading not required.)

Army Form C. 2118.

VOL. I. page 2

Instructions regarding War Diaries and Intelligence Summaries are contained in F.S. Regs., Part II and the Staff Manual respectively. Title pages will be prepared in manuscript.

Hour, Date, Place	Summary of Events and Information	Remarks and references to Appendices
JUNE 20th ctd.	who told him to find a good place himself. He ultimately found Officers Quarters, Officers & Mens billets in CITÉ DIX & a convenient store shed in PLACE GENIN, also with the aid of our tarpaulins we fixed up a rain/proof store. Temporary Field Kitchen arrangt.	
" 21st	Lieut Ferguson organised the inspection of town. Water supply & toilet, latrine conditions of town not good.	
" 24th–30th	I returned to Section having seen methods of Sanitary Officers of 1st, 15th & 16th Divisions. Organised for the inspection of outlying billeting areas MARLES LES MINES, DIVION, RUITZ, 9. MAISNIL. Got out maps of each district, marked in Latrines, Water supplies &c I had Reports on each place, each Latrine being identified by a number. This a Photograph copy of map with Latrines marked in & numbers could be sent to M.O. of unit when any complaints arose about any particular latrine. Some Units worked well at fixing getting despite flystrap latrines in place of shallow trench or bucket system, notable the R.W.Js at MARLES LES MINES. The acting M.O. was LIEUT. WILLIAMS of 135 Field Ambulance. The A & S.H.(11th Batt) did excellent work in BRUAY. Manure disposal is a constant worry as units will not keep abreast of the works once they get behind it seems almost impossible to pick up again & thus piles of manure accumulate in yards. The Divisional Signal Co. have accumulated two such piles in BRUAY.	Capt [signature] O.C. 83rd San. Sec.

83rd SANITARY SECTION.
40th DIVISION.

SECRET

Army Form C. 2118.

WAR DIARY for JULY 1916.
~~INTELLIGENCE SUMMARY~~
VOLUME 2. P.1.

(Erase heading not required.)

Instructions regarding War Diaries and Intelligence Summaries are contained in F.S. Regs., Part II and the Staff Manual respectively. Title pages will be prepared in manuscript.

Hour, Date, Place	Summary of Events and Information	Remarks and references to Appendices
July 1st BRUAY.	The Sanitary Section have supplied a few trap-door latrins-tops to some of the units & these seem to work satisfactorily. H.L.I.'s have been troublesome as they are slack in their Sanitary work.	
" 3rd "	Special inspection of latrines &c in various units in moving. Complaints that certain units have not left things as they should have done. There is of course always a difficulty when a unit moves out about cleaning up everything but in some cases latrine pits were left open & the contents exposed to flies & also buckets were left half full of excreta.	
" 4th BRACQUEMONT	Suspected case of Enteric - a private Beesley No 22406 of 11th KORL (17 Rue de Tulis Mametey) R&DR disinfected (Report sent in to A.D.M.S. 4.VII.6.) Left Bruay in morning for an area in the line, the Division taking over 1st Division Sector or Sub Section of Sgt Carnoli & owner to Lillers & Les Brebis, rest of Section billed at BRACQUEMONT, S. end of NOEUX LES MINES. Section billed, yard & stores at 26 RUE INKERMAN, officer & offices billed at 25 RUE St ARNAUD. 3 lorry loads of material brought from Bruay. Day spent in getting things into order.	
" 5th "	In winding went over to Bruay to get some details of this district as to Cart & fatigues &c as the 1st Division Sanitary officer did the civilian as well as the army scavenging.	
" 6th "	A hard day getting arrangements made about carts, fatigues & "Carts" went to the following communes- Got things at BRACQUEMONT into a kind of working order- Sphinxes will no doubt lead to improvement. Went to LES BREBIS to arrange things there.	
" 7th - 8th "	Carts fatigues had turned up very late.	
" 13th "	My own men were working as a first sweeper along with fatigues in order to get the place into some sort of order. To MINX in morning for wood for Latrine tops (Trap door pattern). Commenced conversion of fly infected bucket latrines into deep pit Fly proof pattern. Trap door tops. Inspected LES BREBIS in afternoon & find that about also it will be possible to convert almost every latrine to the deep trench pattern.	
" 17th "	Case of DIPHTHERIA reported from LES BREBIS, BILLET 632. Pte McKay No 12306- Report sent in to A.D.M.S. after investigation billet disinfected.	

(73989) W4141—463. 400,000. 9/14. H.&J.Ltd. Forms/C. 2118/10.

83rd SANITARY SECTION.
40th DIVISION.

SECRET

WAR DIARY for JULY 1916.

or

INTELLIGENCE SUMMARY. Vol. 2. P. 2.

(Erase heading not required.)

Army Form C. 2118.

Instructions regarding War Diaries and Intelligence Summaries are contained in F.S. Regs., Part II and the Staff Manual respectively. Title pages will be prepared in manuscript.

Hour, Date, Place	Summary of Events and Information	Remarks and references to Appendices
July 14th BRACQUEMONT.	To MINY in morning to fetch wood for more latrine tops. 10 have been made & supplied so far. LES BREBIS. in afternoon for wire for hingis of latrine tops & for cement barrels for refuse tubs in the streets of BRACQUEMONT. Stacking of the manure is progressing at LES BREBIS. with the aid of a fatigue of 30 men from 121st Batt. The earth covering done by last division is built up insufficient as a preventive against fly-breeding & flies are hatching out readily. Stacks are to be sprayed with strong cresol (about 1 part in 7).	
" 15th "	Very two or three days. Visited DROUVIN & HAILLICOURT.	
" 16th "	To Divisional Laundry, BETHUNE, where two of the section men are stationed looking after disinfection. Took new asphalt latrine top & some bin-fireable wood.	
" 17th "	Took Pte CAZEAU to DROUVIN to test water supply for 51st Mobile Vet. Section. 9 also to HOUCHIN to test water supply from a well used by No 93 Coy. D.A.C. 3 means water. Advised another supply which is good water. Mapped out DROUVIN & HOUCHIN. Advised M.O. of D.A.C. at latter place to commence conversion of shallow bucket system of latrines into deep pit fly-proof type pattern. In afternoon visited trenches at CALONNE & inspected latrines in No 1 sector. At least 2 bucket latrines still to be converted. Sgt admitted to hospital suffering from various breakdown.	
" 19th "	Case of MILD SCARLET FEVER in 20th MX Regt notified today. Billet disinfected & report sent in to A.D.M.S. Visited FOSSE No 2 de NEUX district & arranged with O.C. Wagon Lines B. Batt. 185 Regt R.F.A. about conversion of latrines in his area. Inspected area occupied by D. Batt 188 & 185. also No 1 Police Post.	
" 22nd "	In afternoon to CALONNE area.	
" 24th "	Made arrangements about water supply for a water cart to water men at use of BRACQUEMONT.	
" 25th "	Made out maps of CALONNE. BULLY GRENAY. GRENAY & MAROC. Case of German measles reported in afternoon. Officer of B. Batt 188 & 185 R.F.A. (Major LEGGETT) Billet disinfected. To MINY for more wood for latrine tops. Inspection of BRACQUEMONT district	Frank Jeffs Capt S.C.
" 26th "	in afternoon. My fatigue men reduced by 3 by A.A.Q.M.G. to economies. Difficulties in disposing rubbish dump at LES BREBIS. chiefly owing to civilians	

83rd SANITARY SECTION.
40th DIVISION.

SECRET

WAR DIARY for July. 1916.

INTELLIGENCE SUMMARY. Vol. 2. p. 3

Army Form C. 2118.

(Erase heading not required.)

Instructions regarding War Diaries and Intelligence Summaries are contained in F.S. Regs., Part II and the Staff Manual respectively. Title pages will be prepared in manuscript.

Hour, Date, Place	Summary of Events and Information	Remarks and references to Appendices
July. 26th. Noted.	dumping refuse there which ought to be burnt. Ordered that the place should be frequently sprayed with strong cresol.	
" 27th. BRACQUEMONT	Water cart on the main road for first time this afternoon. Horse lances. Drivers supplied by 137th Field Ambulance. 6/Cpl Thomas i/c.	
" 28th "	Requested from A.A.&Q.M.G. a special fatigue to get rubbish dump at LES BREBIS into order. No fatigues available – would require a large fatigue for several days.	
" 29th "	With Col. Moore (A.A.&Q.M.G.) to LES BREBIS to see rubbish dump. No fatigues forthcoming. Wrote report on the dump to A.D.M.S. refusing to take responsibility for it unless I could have assistance to get & keep it in order.	
" 30th "	HOUCHIN in afternoon to report upon whether any soldiers were billeted in houses where DIPHTHERIA had been reported. Investigated matter & came to conclusion that so called DIPHTHERIA was TONSILITIS. Reported to A.D.M.S.	

40th Divn.

83rd Sanitary Section

August 1916

COMMITTEE FOR THE
MEDICAL HISTORY OF THE WAR
Date -9 OCT 1915

SANITARY SECTION 83.
40th Division

Search

Army Form C. 2118.

WAR DIARY for AUGUST 1916
or
INTELLIGENCE SUMMARY. Vol III. Ø'.
(Erase heading not required.)

Instructions regarding War Diaries and Intelligence Summaries are contained in F.S. Regs., Part II and the Staff Manual respectively. Title pages will be prepared in manuscript.

Hour, Date, Place	Summary of Events and Information	Remarks and references to Appendices
Aug 1st & 2nd Bracquemont.	Mainly office work, writing up monthly report.	
3rd	HOUCHIN, DROUVIN & HALLICOURT:- Shed school at first place disinfected by one of my Sanitary Inspectors with a view to the Tonsilitis mentioned in diary on July 30th.	
5th	In afternoon Bussy GRENAY & GRENAY. inspecting billets, latrines &c. Ended about LES BREBIS.	
7th	LES BREBIS in afternoon to investigate complaints as to civilian latrines reported by M.O. 13th Yorks. Interviewed Town Major with a view to getting things put right.	
8th	HOUCHIN in afternoon to investigate a public nuisance caused by a civilian who keeps pigs & has briefly a fowl lying about - made notes for report on subject. Later examined an overflowing sump-pit on grounds of 137th Field Ambulance. Sump-pit to be for waste water from baths & incidently requires to be remade. Advised that Pit to be called in.	
9th	LES BREBIS in afternoon General inspection of billets &c.	
10th	Examined peace broke DISTILLERY on HERSIN ROAD, where waste liquor from distillery is turned out into large open pits. Hitherto this has been regarded as an 16th Divisional area. Went with D.A.D.M.S (Sanitary) of the Corps. Saw: Officer 16th Div. Rose to swarming with fly larvæ (musca DOMESTICA & LUCILIA or CALLIPHORA - or both.) Applied to S.S.O. for 20 galls paraffin to treat the pits. Experimenting in evening with 1 pit using 5 balls paraffin diluted to a 20% Solⁿ with water. This brought larvæ to surface. Tried burning off the surface with dry grass & the paraffin. Put quick lime on to two of the pits at distillery.	
11th	"C" Solⁿ & also same strengths of cresol on heaps of horse manure 4'×4'×1'6" high. Continuing treatment of distillery pits with quick lime. Result of experimenting on horse manure shows that cresol is more efficacious than "C" Solⁿ. 2 Galls per heap were used. Many larvæ were dead in all the heaps while the control heaps only treated with water swarmed with larvæ. The 20% cresol had killed almost all larvæ i.e. only 2 or 3 were discovered after diligent search. The 5% cresol was much more efficient than the 5% "C" Solution. I think the explanation is that the "C" Solⁿ will not mix with water, so found unevenly from the water cart. Some patches of mix with water, the manure getting little else than water.	

SANITARY SECTION 83.
40th Division

Secret

Army Form C. 2118.

WAR DIARY for August 1916

INTELLIGENCE SUMMARY. Vol III p. 2

(Erase heading not required.)

Hour, Date, Place	Summary of Events and Information	Remarks and references to Appendices
Aug 12th BARLINMONT	In afternoon to HOUCHIN to report on case of DIPHTHERIA. Report sent in. Case at least 10 days ago & almost certainly only tonsillitis.	
13th	Capt Browne took ill on this date & went into hospital the following day	
15th	On this date Lieut George Morris, R.A.M.C. 83rd Sanitary Section, 40th Division, reported to A.D.M.S. who gave an idea of work reqd & suggested that he found suitable Headquarters of Section should be moved to Nœux les Mines where most of its work is required. Went over books of Section & checked imprest account taking over 87 francs 30 centimes which was amount shown on the books. Also wrote to A.D.M.S. explaining that I had taken over & that all was correct. Had system of working explained by S/Sgt Lindsay & went to several billets where latrines were necessary & got them under way. In afternoon went to LES BREBIS & interviewed the Town Major. He offered every help to the Section & promised to find a suitable place in Les Brebis for Head Qrs. Inspected Rubbish & Manure Dumps at Les Brebis. Manure Dumps in a very untidy condition in spite of the little labour available. Rubbish Dumps went to fatigue parts.	
16th	Inspected place beside DETHUNEY on KERAN Road where the state layout was very offensive still. On going up to the line which had been put on the surface the larvæ were found in great numbers underneath.	
Aug 17.F.	Went to LES BREBIS and fixed up a Headquarters with the Town Major. Got billets for officers & 36 men including fatigues, a store, a workshop. Permission to erect a tent for an office, & a shed for Cook house & dining hall.	

SANITARY SECTION 83
HOLL Division
Search

Army Form C. 2118.

WAR DIARY
for August 1916

INTELLIGENCE SUMMARY. Vol III p.3

(Erase heading not required.)

Instructions regarding War Diaries and Intelligence Summaries are contained in F.S. Regs., Part II. and the Staff Manual respectively. Title pages will be prepared in manuscript.

Hour, Date, Place	Summary of Events and Information	Remarks and references to Appendices
Aug. 17th BRACQUEMONT	Inspected French Soldiers latrine at PETIT SAINS, condemned it, gave instructions to fill it in & to dig a new one of deep trench type. Inspected billet of 283 R.E. & found a nuisance caused by waste water & drawing from gutter from a pig sty. Also inspected a similar nuisance at Billets 145 to 147 at Petit Sains. Wrote to French Maires about these matters. In afternoon sent men & materials to 165 BR.B/S. to clean out billets & erect hut washhouse. Found Interpreter with his aid arranged that nuisance at 283 R.E.'s billet should be removed. Indented for some wood for the building of the shed & sent party off to collect that & continue to work at 165 BR.B/S.	
" 14.		
" 15th	Moved up all stores & equipment necessary to La Brebis in two loads by the lorry. Transferred the main part of personnel so that now La Brebis became Head Quarters. Bracquemont was left in charge of a Sergeant.	
" 20th LES BREBIS	Personnel not engaged in inspecting mainly employed arranging stores & Commenced building a store at back of billet. Carried on with Establishment of Head Qrs. here. Was in consultation with A.D.M.S. re improvements at La Brebis & Calonne. Arranged to have men working always at Calonne & visit Sections. Noeux-les-Mallicourt only once a week. Arranged to fit up rubbish dumps in concert with Town Mayor. Commenced Parades at 6.30 a.m. Fatigue men forms alternating charge of inspectors to clean La Brebis. Parade again at 8.15 am when every obtained permission to have 2 civilian Carts to work defects are collected several barrels & large number of tins from R.E. & Q.M. stores respectively to be used for civilian rubbish. These were caused	
" 22nd		

SANITARY SECTION 83
40th Division

Secret

WAR DIARY for AUGUST 1916.
INTELLIGENCE SUMMARY. Vol III. p.4.
(Erase heading not required.)

Army Form C. 2118.

Instructions regarding War Diaries and Intelligence Summaries are contained in F.S. Regs., Part II. and the Staff Manual respectively. Title pages will be prepared in manuscript.

Hour, Date, Place	Summary of Events and Information	Remarks and references to Appendices
Aug. 22nd. HS BRKBIS.	Properly labelled. Visited Calonne & inspected it in general. N.Os have had great difficulty in dealing with tins & rubbish which have to be buried. Latrines in good condition. Arranged to send up an inspector each day, he to find out best method of working that district. Captain T.E. Shand R.B.M.C. (S.R.) took over the Command of Bde Sanitary Section.	
25th "	Visited Calonne and inspected the place generally, much requires to be done here. Much ground invaded by indiscriminate dumping of dead rubbish, in every corner, & the digging of small latrine trenches. Old refuse dumps had condition. New refuse dumps good condition & good site. Rde generally requires much attention at Bracquemont. Saw Sergeants in charge.	
26 "	Civilian grounds at back of D.I.D.O.S. disgraceful condition. Wrote town Mayor (Noeuples. Mines) as also walls. Re arranged working of incinerators. Pte Gray has been put in Charge of Calonne Bully Grenay. He has with him 3/6 M.H.R.	
Aug. 28 "	The N.C.O. & 4 other ranks reported here for duty (P.B. men). Saw Town Mayor re new site (Sanitary Section) moving from present site. Typed on new site which is an improvement.	
" 29 "	Ten men commenced cleaning up new site. Section Parade 6am. Instructed the men, as regards the duties & what was expected of them. Medical Board inspection of P.B. T.U. men at 2.30pm at Zen Brebis & at 10.15am at Bracquemont. Condemned about 40 wooden barrels.	

SANITARY SECTION 83
11th Division

Secret

Army Form C. 2118.

WAR DIARY for AUGUST 1916.
or
INTELLIGENCE SUMMARY. Vol III. p 445

(Erase heading not required.)

Instructions regarding War Diaries and Intelligence Summaries are contained in F. S. Regs., Part II. and the Staff Manual respectively. Title pages will be prepared in manuscript.

Hour, Date, Place	Summary of Events and Information	Remarks and references to Appendices
Aug. 29th reS. 26.b.35.	At Calonne, which were being used for storing water. They were in a very foul, stagnant state. At "Dug Out" at Les Brebis has been used as a latrine. This has been cleaned & put out of Bounds by the Town Major. Two Privates (act NCOs) reported here for duty from 2nd London Sanitary Coy.	
31st. "	At Bracquemont. arranged with A.D.M.S. 10th Division to visit & report on water supply. Saw several nuisance principally manure heaps, arranged for their treatment & removal. Several cesspits in bad condition, Town Major being written to re these.	

B. Shaw Coyt
W.D.S.
11th Division

140/134

40th Divn.

83rd Sanitary Section

Sept 1916

COMMITTEE FOR THE
MEDICAL HISTORY OF THE WAR
Date 30 OCT. 1916

SECRET

Vol IV

WAR DIARY of 83rd Sanitary Section
40th Division

INTELLIGENCE SUMMARY.

(Erase heading not required.)

Army Form C. 2118.

Instructions regarding War Diaries and Intelligence Summaries are contained in F.S. Regs., Part II and the Staff Manual respectively. Title pages will be prepared in manuscript.

Hour, Date, Place	Summary of Events and Information	Remarks and references to Appendices
1st September 1916. Map Reference Sheet 36B France 1:40,000 2nd Edition L.35.B.68.	Visited foos at request of A.D.M.S. to report on water supply. Special report sent to A.D.M.S. by 4 pm today re this water supply. No 4 premises at foo Brebis moved to Rue Haymark Les Brebis. Map reference Sheet 36.B. France 1:40,000 3rd Edition L.35.B.68.	
3rd Sept. 1916.	Monthly report sent to A.D.M.S. 40th Division. Special visit to Refuse dumps and incinerators in LES BREBIS. Old refuse dump being cleaned & filled. New refuse dump in good condition & I think this the one is sufficient for some months.	
4th Sept 1916	Cpl. Gray has been put in charge of hoos area, and Pte Files is to do Maroc area, while Pte Hanves is doing Special work (Map tracing) at the office.	
5th Sept 1916.	Visited Bethune (Laundry) DROUVIN, HAILLICOURT, & HOUCHIN. Special report rendered to A.D.M.S. 40 the Division re the visit Two Privates (3167 Pte SHACKELL W. & 3148 Pte DURANT. F.H from 2nd London Sanitary Coy R.A.M.C.) reported here for duty & have been taken on the strength accordingly.	
6th Sept. 1916	Went round with the M.O. of 20th Middlesex. LES BREBS the area occupied by the Battalion. He is to dig 6 new urinals & 9 one new latrine.	
7th Sept 1916.	Fatigue Men at Bracquemont (P.B.& T.4) are now being billeted & food cooked at Section Yard 3 under control of the Sgt. Visited BRACQUEMONT. Saw A.D.M.S. 40th Division & water-cart inspection etc. Inspected some urinals & action was taken.	

SECRET.

Vol IV

WAR DIARY of 93rd Sanitary Section
or
INTELLIGENCE SUMMARY.

Army Form C. 2118.

40th Division

(Erase heading not required.)

Instructions regarding War Diaries and Intelligence Summaries are contained in F.S. Regs., Part II and the Staff Manual respectively. Title pages will be prepared in manuscript.

Hour, Date, Place	Summary of Events and Information	Remarks and references to Appendices
8th September 1916.	Visited Loos & inspected generally the district. Arranged with Camp Commandant to billet & ration Cpl Gray, whom I have left in charge of this area. The wells in this district are not satisfactory. I trust that pumps will be supplied to these wells. I tested 3 wells (Nernsts test) all are suitable if pumps were of bleaching powder is evident to watercart.	
9th Sept 1916.	Extended Conference at 8 Field Ambulance Noeux-les-Mines.	
10th Sept 1916.	Visited A.D.M.S. 40th Division & asked for two more sets of Horrocks Test Box. Have to borrow from 135 & 137 F. Ambulance. Three P.B. men detailed to report to Soup Kitchen 173 ADC for duty. Authority O.C. 40th Divisional Coy.	
11th Sept 1916.	Authority O.C. 40th Divisional Coy.	
12th Oct 1916.	2/C SHACKELL N. 2nd London Sanitary Coy was detailed to report to A.D.M.S. 33rd Division for Sanitary duty (Authority ADMS 40th Division).	
12:15 p.m.	Was visited by M.O. 12th S.W.B. who said that both he & the M.O. 20th Middlesex had condemned their Qr. Stores as insanitary. I immediately paid a visit accompanied by the M.O. 12 S.W.B. & my no pastor. On inspection I found that the place was very untidy. No attempt had been made to have the place clean. I pointed out several defects of their surroundings. As far as this sections work is concerned I cannot find anything wrong in my opinion the place was in as good a sanitary condition I pointed out several items which they have to do to remedy the state of affairs. They whole trouble arises from the fact that they look after the stores and careful enough & they leave a new area without a thought for those coming in.	

SECRET

Vol IV

WAR DIARY of 83rd Sanitary Section
40th Division
INTELLIGENCE SUMMARY.

Army Form C. 2118.

(Erase heading not required.)

Hour, Date, Place	Summary of Events and Information	Remarks and references to Appendices
14th September 1916.	Visited A.D.M.S. 40th Division. Also went round & saw several Sanitary defects.	
16th September 1916.	Visited A.D.M.S. 40th Division. Accompanied the Sergt Inspector round part of BRACQUEMONT district. Punishment Dr. Holey E.N. (M.T.) deprived of one days pay for being absent without leave from Roll Call 9.p.m until he reported at 9.15 p.m (fifteen minutes).	
19th Sept. 1916.	Visited A.D.M.S. 40th Division. Attended funeral of fellow of the late Capt Straw R.A.M.C.	
20th Sept. 1916.	Visited Conference of Sanitary Officers at D.M.S. office LILLERS.	
22nd Sept. 1916.	Visited La Gorgue for the purpose of visiting 61st Divisional Sanitary Section.	
23rd Sept. 1916.	Visited WOOS & saw many parts of the district. Special report rendered to A.D.M.S. 40th Division re water supply to Battalion areas.	
25th Sept. 1916.	Visited PETIT SAINS & made a general Sanitary Survey.	
26th Sept. 1916.	Spent whole day at BRACQUEMONT & went round district with the Sergeant. District generally so in fairly good condition.	
27th Sept 1916.	Visited MAROC. Area generally so clean & tidy.	
29th Sept. 1916.	Visited Divisional Laundry, DROUVIN, HOUCHIN & HAILLICOURT areas, reasonably clean & tidy.	

T. Jilland
Capt.
R.A.M.C.

O.C. Sanitary Section
40th Division

140/1815

40th Divn

83rd Sanitary Section

Brigade

COMMITTEE FOR THE
MEDICAL HISTORY OF THE WAR
Date -9 DEC. 1916

Vol V.

WAR DIARY
or
INTELLIGENCE SUMMARY.

of 63 Sanitary Section. for Month of October 1916

Army Form C. 2118.

(Erase heading not required.)

Hour, Date, Place	Summary of Events and Information	Remarks and references to Appendices
1st October 1916. L.35.13.1.9.	Visited Beuvry (PETIT SAINS) & examined a very sick old Inspector. The child appeared to be suffering from Interrupted Pneumonia & advanced Tuberculosis of Lungs. As there were no more British Service hospitals in the Terrane I told the mother that she must inform the MAIRE & get the child taken to hospital at once, as the child was showing dangerous signs. The child died before it could be removed. I have had the house thoroughly disinfected & measures also made. NOEUX for the purpose of washing linen. Also visited the Casa of Scarlet Fever in No. 2 Section (Sgt. KITTLE) 5 Siege Battery R.E.A. I recommended as the children in the same thoroughly & also scarce bathing the adults. but there was no the slightest sign of Scarlet Fever in the house. The names disinfection of rooms & clothing was also inspected. Latrines & urinals for 8 farms also inspected. Spent on work for NOEUX area.	
2nd October 1916.	Visited MAZINGARBE & inspected Chateau temporary Hosp. 170 Brigade. The Chateau grounds are very fit for being Sanitary. An Inspector has been placed in charge to	

WAR DIARY of 83 Sanitary Section.

INTELLIGENCE SUMMARY.

Army Form C. 2118.

(Erase heading not required.)

Instructions regarding War Diaries and Intelligence Summaries are contained in F.S. Regs., Part II. and the Staff Manual respectively. Title pages will be prepared in manuscript.

Hour, Date, Place	Summary of Events and Information	Remarks and references to Appendices
2 October 1916 Calais	Supervised & carried out various assignments. Also inspected various latrines & urinals for information for report. Visited NOEUX & Twenty South, inspecting Latrines & Urinals. Visited BRAQUEMONT & went round part of area with the Sergeant Inspector.	
L.35.B.1.9. 3rd October 1916 "	Visited LOOS. Area is undergoing changes, as are permanent & half supplies for the Battalion area is "in the way". I hope to have the "tanks" filled up shortly.	
5th October 1916.	Visited PETIT SAINS. Saw several parts of the district appeared the latrines, which the Town Major showed me & report saying that they were inadequate & required immediate attention. As the latrine accommodation is at least 470 in this area, it is ample. The Officer who reported this, appearing to the Town Major knows, saw only 2 latrines, whereas he saw about 14 deep Trenches, with over 30 bores & flaps. I showed the Town Major our own ways of making the various latrines. As regards of Assistant of 14th A.S. Highlanders I made this Camp at HAZINGARBE. Specific report was included in the Specific report on latrines & Incinerators.	

WAR DIARY of F3 Pauling Column

INTELLIGENCE SUMMARY.

Army Form C. 2118.

Instructions regarding War Diaries and Intelligence Summaries are contained in F.S. Regs., Part II. and the Staff Manual respectively. Title pages will be prepared in manuscript.

(Erase heading not required.)

Hour, Date, Place	Summary of Events and Information	Remarks and references to Appendices
5th October 1916 (contd)	It relating is heard on the 170s, the regiments of the 40th Division who carry out suggestions made to them & repeating carrying out the items of the attached Memorandum.	
L.35. B.I.9.	No 28. Dated 12 April 1916 – Sanitation – Lines trans whenever they get into another divisional area, it is found that there has not been the slightest attempt made to remedy with this Memorandum.	
6th October 1916.	Visited MAZINGARBE. Found that 6 good latrine pits had been dug, also urinals & refuse pits.	
9th October 1916.	Visited MAZINGARBE. Good progress has been made in the requirements in the Northern trench.	
10th October 1916.	Visited BARQUEROIT. Saw several parts of the area. It is also being kept in a reasonable good condition.	
12th October 1916.	Visited MAZINGARBE & PHILOSOPHE for the purpose of immediately seeing defects which ought to be remedied at once. The N.C.O. & 20th Londons (P/3 men) reported for this duty.	
14th October 1916.	Visited PHILOSOPHE with Inspector to see character for sanitary report on PHILOSOPHE. Also made PETIT SAINS for Sanitary report on PHILOSOPHE. This area is in a reasonable condition	

WAR DIARY of S.S. Sanitary Section

Army Form C. 2118.

(Erase heading not required.)

Hour, Date, Place	Summary of Events and Information	Remarks and references to Appendices
15th October 1916 L.35.B.1.9	Visited BRAQUEMONT for the purpose of investigating into the case of Diphtheria then occurring in civilian homes. The patient who died was buried on the Saturday 14th. Another case of illness in same home. Another case was seen in same street. The patient being in bed obviously ill. Some OR. cases of illness in same street. Diagnosis uncertain. No British soldiers were billeted in the homes, but I thought it advisable to have all bedding removed from the street belonging to A.S.C. & R.E. I saw the Officers & the men were immediately removed. The infected huts were thoroughly disinfected & recolourwashed. In the room were also sprayed. Inmates were told to cleanse them thoroughly. Privy middens are also sprayed & are to be emptied. The Road — Rue de la Marticipir was put out of bounds to soldiers. D.R.O. 679. Public notices were placed under the above before forbidding the drawing of water. Visited BRAQUEMONT, SAUCHY LESTRÉE, BETHUNE, DROUVIN, HOUCHIN, SAILLIECHOT. District Sanitary in fair condition.	
16th October 1916.		

WAR DIARY or INTELLIGENCE SUMMARY

Army Form C. 2118.

83 Sanitary Section

(Erase heading not required.)

Hour, Date, Place	Summary of Events and Information	Remarks and references to Appendices
17th October 1916. L.35.B.1.9	Two NCOs. & 19 other ranks (R.A.M.C. 135 F.A.) reported for Sanitary duty at MAZINGARBE. They were individually put on 65 day trench latrine. Spent whole day at MAZINGARBE saw the work now in hand & next round the 10 other huts with M.O. 21 Middlesex & arranged for their latrines & urinals to the fires up. Four carpenters reported for duty in Sailor Workshop they are being employed in making box latrines. Saw work in progress. Visited QUALITY STREET. 6 urinalspits being made. In afternoon visited MAZRO for purpose of individually dosing C.S.M. Guiseppi. The 6 controls were individually sent to 135 F.A. & now of A.D.M.S. & the 5 rest were through of sprays. All the Case was sent down last night, as a suspected case of C.Meningitis. the 5 controls were sent to 135 F.A. of the day out disinfected. There was no connection between these two cases.	
18th October 1916.		

WAR DIARY L3 Sanitary Section

Army Form C. 2118.

INTELLIGENCE SUMMARY.

(Erase heading not required.)

Hour, Date, Place	Summary of Events and Information	Remarks and references to Appendices
20th October 1916. L.35.B.1.9	Visited BRAQUEMONT. Saw some parts of the district, also issued a load of boxes for labour making.	
21st October 1916.	Our Carpenter left at 12 noon and said that they were not going to return again. Gave one my Inspector asking N.C.O. noted [illegible]	
23 October 1916.	Visited BRAQUEMONT. Two P.B. men reported for duty.	
24th October 1916.	Monthly report rendered to A.D.M.S. 40th Division. 1 N.C.O. returned from Divisional Laundry for duty with Section. 1 N.C.O. from 41st Sanitary Section returns to K.	
25th October 1916.	Visited BRAQUEMONT. Saw round parts of district. M N.C.O. returned from German Prisoners Camp HOUCHIN for duty with section. M. N.C.O. 41st Sanitary Section returns to him. A.D.M.S. 14 Corps visited today. Look this over some parts of district LESBRSAIS, also at MAZINGARBE. Sgt Fay o Cpl BATLEY reported here for duty from LOOS. M. N.C.O. 21 L.T. 60 Sanitary Sect. Two N.COs o 19 Other Ranks (A.O.M.C. 135 F.A) reported back to 135 F.A for duty.	

WAR DIARY
83 Sanitary Section
INTELLIGENCE SUMMARY

Army Form C. 2118.

Hour, Date, Place	Summary of Events and Information	Remarks and references to Appendices
26th October 1916 L.35.B.1.9.	Advance Party (Capt. BRAMSHOTT. & arranged for the establishment at billets (Section) to be brought up to HESDIGNEUL.	
27th October 1916	Twenty two NCOs & Other ranks (Sanitary Section) joined 135 F.A. in accordance with 46th Division R.A.M.C. Operation order No 6. Personnel of 141 Sanitary Section arrived & took over premises at HESBAS also MAZINGARBE	
28th October 1916 Map Reference 36B. S.11.C.1.1.	Left HESBREAS at 9.40 with 3 Ton Lorry & 5 NCO & men and FODEN disinfector at DIVISIONAL HQ of the Proceeded through BETHUNE BRUAY to St Pol & ROELLECOURT Billeted for the night at St. POL.	
29 October 1916. Map Reference 36B. T.9.D.2.5.	Joined 135 F.A. in morning at ROCOURT.	
31st October 1916	Visited ROELLECOURT & Saw A.D.M.S. Saw Sanitary parts of the area & arranged for some improvements to be proceeded with at once.	Lt. T. G. Sheard. O.C. 83rd Sanitary Section.

40/1262

40th Div.

83rd Sanitary Section

Nov 1916

COMMITTEE FOR THE
MEDICAL HISTORY OF THE WAR

Date -3 JAN. 1917

Sent

WAR DIARY
or
INTELLIGENCE SUMMARY.

Army Form C. 2118.

P. & 3 Sanitary Section
Vol. VI. Page 1.

(Erase heading not required.)

Hour, Date, Place	Summary of Events and Information	Remarks and references to Appendices
1 November 1916. ROCOURT E2 France 1:10,000 Lens	Visited ROEULECOURT & detailed all sanitary men to commence dig latrines & refuse pits & to clean up area. During the day 5 latrine trenches, 3 refuse pits & 4 temporary urinals were completed as well as pails & emptied, cleaned & put away. Refuse collected & burned.	
2 November 1916. Lens 1:10,000 SIBIVILLE D 3. France	Left ROCOURT with 135 Field Ambulance for SIBIVILLE. Immediately on starting the Force Douglasflin lorry stuck in the mud. It took 5 hours before we got it out again. We found the 135 Field Ambulance at SIBIVILLE.	
3 November 1916.	Inspectors were sent round to arrange details including REBREUVE. Several latrines & refuse pits were seen in course of construction. No fixed latrine system is proposed round this area.	
4 November 1916. France Lens 1:10,000 VILLERS l'HOPITAL C 4	Left SIBIVILLE with 135 Field Ambulance & arrived at VILLERS L'HOPITAL.	

SECRET.

Army Form C. 2118.

WAR DIARY
83 Sanitary Section
Vol VI Page 2

or

INTELLIGENCE SUMMARY.

(Erase heading not required.)

Instructions regarding War Diaries and Intelligence Summaries are contained in F.S. Regs., Part II and the Staff Manual respectively. Title pages will be prepared in manuscript.

Hour, Date, Place	Summary of Events and Information	Remarks and references to Appendices
5 November 1916. Army 10000 Corps LANCHES BS.	Left VILLERS L'HOPITAL with 135 F.A. & arrived at LANCHES. Via FROHEN- GRAND FROHEN PETIT MEILLARD BERNAVILLE DORMESMONT.	
6 November 1916.	Visited BERNAVILLE & ordered 3 NCO (San Sect.) to make sanitary survey of the district.	
7 November 1916.	Visited BERNAVILLE saw the work in progress.	
8th November 1916. France 10000 Corps BERNAVILLE BS.	In accordance with instructions received from ADMS. I took up residence at BERNAVILLE & one P Gunter (San Sect) reported for temporary duty with Town Major BIERNAVILLE	
9th November 1916.	Visited RIBEAUCOURT for purpose of investigating case of German measles	

SECRET.

WAR DIARY 8 & Burley Cashing Army Form C. 2118.
or
INTELLIGENCE SUMMARY. vol vi page 3

(Erase heading not required.)

Instructions regarding War Diaries and Intelligence Summaries are contained in F.S. Regs., Part II and the Staff Manual respectively. Title pages will be prepared in manuscript.

Hour, Date, Place	Summary of Events and Information	Remarks and references to Appendices
13 November 1916	Visited CANDAS. for purpose of inoculating Case of Hyperemia	
15 November 1916. France 10:00 O4.	Left BERNAVILLE with 13 F.A. & arrived at MEZEROLLES	
16 November 1916	Visited FROHEN LE GRAND, & arranged for 6 NCO's (Sam Sect.) to make a Sanitary Survey of area	
17 November 1916. France 10:00 F4.	Left MEZEROLLES & arrived at BOUQUEMAISON.	
22 November 1916. France 10:00 E5.	Left BOUQUEMAISON. & arrived at DOULLENS	

SECRET.

Army Form C. 2118.

W.B. Stanley Archer
Vol. VI page 4

WAR DIARY
or
INTELLIGENCE SUMMARY.
(Erase heading not required.)

Instructions regarding War Diaries and Intelligence Summaries are contained in F.S. Regs., Part II. and the Staff Manual respectively. Title pages will be prepared in manuscript.

Hour, Date, Place	Summary of Events and Information	Remarks and references to Appendices
23 November 1916. Jaime Lens 1000yds CANAPLES C6	Left DOULLENS & arrived at CANAPLES.	
24 November 1916. France Abbeville 1000yds L6	Left CANAPLES & arrived at AILLY & H. CLOCHER.	
25th November 1916	Granted leave of absence from 27th November to 6th December. (Authority ADMS 40th Division). Lieut J.K. DAVIES arrived & took over charge of Section. Handed over F.2.0 - Imprest account. Took over from Capt T.G. Shaw Sanitary Section were handed over 90 Francs - Imprest account. (J.K.Davies)	
26th November 1916	Inspected the billeting area at AILLY-LE HT CLOCHER & found it to be in a bad condition. Gave instructions to have all the publich closed away & burnt. Commenced converting pail latrines	

Army Form C. 2118.

WAR DIARY of 83 Sanitary Section
or
INTELLIGENCE SUMMARY.

VOL VI page 5

(Erase heading not required.)

Hour, Date, Place	Summary of Events and Information	Remarks and references to Appendices
27th November 1916.	which were previously into deep pits. Sent three inspectors one to each Brigade HdQrs to supervise the sanitation of Brigade Hd Qrs & three units who were without N.C.O. afterwards to look after sanitation of units.	
28th November 1916	Completed two deep pit latrines with two box seats each. Also arranged for the disposal of all manure & infected units. Sent 8 inspectors to inspect the sanitation of the units of the 120th & 721st Bde. one inspector to examine water-carts for deficiencies. Inspected the billets & of 12th & 10th the Regt	
29th November 1916	Sent out inspector to supervise the sanitation of the AUC Brigade also to put water supply of the Regt	
30th November 1916	Inspected billets &c of 120th T.M.B. & 120 M.G. Coy.	J. Davis, A/Capt No C 83 Sanitary Section

Confidential.

War Diary

of

83rd Sanitary Section.

From Dec 1st. — To Dec 31st
1916.

Volume VII

Committee for the Medical History of the War — Date 31 Jan. 1917

SECRET.

WAR DIARY *or* **INTELLIGENCE SUMMARY.**

Army Form C. 2118.

No 83 Sanitary Section Vol VII page 1.

Hour, Date, Place	Summary of Events and Information	Remarks and references to Appendices
1st December 1916 AILLY-LE-Ht CLOCHER France 1/100000 ABBEVILLE L.6.	Visited BELLANCOURT, VAUCHELLES-LES-QUESNY, EPAGNE, EAUCOURT, and PONT REMY, & examined the Sanitation of the units of the 119th Brigade	
2nd December 1916	YZEUX/YONCOURT - BUSSUS. & inspected the Sanitary arrangements of the villages & of the 1st A.S.H.	
3rd December 1916	Sent out 6 inspectors to commence a sanitary survey of all the villages in the area.	
5th December 1916	The inspectors went out & completed the sanitary survey.	
6th December 1916	Visited Yzeuxcourt & inspected billets of 229 Fd Coy. R.E. A/Cpl Gray left for CHATHAM to take up a course of instruction with view to taking up a Temp?y Commission in the R.E. (Authority A.S. GHQ No A/818 dated 26/11/16)	
7th Dec. 1916.	Visited Brucamps & inspected sanitary arrangements of 2/8th Middlesex Regt.	

SECRET

WAR DIARY
or
INTELLIGENCE SUMMARY.
(Erase heading not required.)

Army Form C. 2118.

83 Sanitary Section
Vol. VII page 2.

Instructions regarding War Diaries and Intelligence Summaries are contained in F. S. Regs., Part II and the Staff Manual respectively. Title pages will be prepared in manuscript.

Hour, Date, Place	Summary of Events and Information	Remarks and references to Appendices
8th Dec 1916.	Capt. T.G. Shand returned from leave. Handed over to Capt Shand, 6l20. 1070 francs Imprest account. Took over charge of L Section from Lieut. J.K. DAVIES. & also received 100 francs Imprest account (T.G.Shand)	
11th Dec. 1916.	Began a Sanitary Inspection of the area occupied by 40th Division. Good progress has been made by the different units in the matter of permanent ablution arrangements.	
12th Dec 1916.	Visited VAUCOURT. & inspected Sanitary arrangements.	
1st Dec. 1916. map reference travel 15000 Amiens H36 CHIPILLY.	Sapr. Ailly L.H. CLOCHER marched to PONT REMY entraining there & marched to CHIPILLY.	

SECRET

WAR DIARY D.83 Sanitary Section Army Form C. 2118.
or
INTELLIGENCE SUMMARY. Vol. VII Page 3.

(Erase heading not required.)

Instructions regarding War Diaries and Intelligence Summaries are contained in F.S. Regs., Part II. and the Staff Manual respectively. Title pages will be prepared in manuscript.

Hour, Date, Place	Summary of Events and Information	Remarks and references to Appendices
17th December 1916.	Visited Camps 111 - 112. Made a Sanitary Survey. Letter with suggestions for improvement sent to Staff Captain 120th Brigade.	
18th December 1916.	Visited SAILLY LAURETTE & made inspection of part of district & also water points. Visited Camp 12 & made a Sanitary Inspection of camp. Letter with suggestions for improvement sent to Staff Captain 119 & 121st Brigades	
19th December 1916.	Visited Camps 11 & 13. Made a Sanitary inspection.	
20th December 1916.	Visited Camp 12. Sgt CORNISH A.E. left for England to take up a Commission in Infantry. to see Rutherfords works Authority HQ 40th Division 48 9(A) ADMS. also	
22 December 1916.	Visited Camp 17 at/near B.16 Central (France 1:40,000 Water Point at B.16 Central (Albert) East of MAUREPAS. Several improvements to be instituted as the works permit, when it is taken over by 40th Division.	

SECRET.

WAR DIARY
or
INTELLIGENCE SUMMARY.
(Erase heading not required.)

Army Form C. 2118.

No. 83 Sanitary Section   Vol VII   page 4

Instructions regarding War Diaries and Intelligence Summaries are contained in F.S. Regs., Part II. and the Staff Manual respectively. Title pages will be prepared in manuscript.

Hour, Date, Place	Summary of Events and Information	Remarks and references to Appendices
23rd November 1916.	Visited Camp 13 to see purpose of Sanitary arrangements	
26th November 1916.	Visited Camp 12 & inspected sanitary arrangements	
26th November 1916	Visited BRAY for purpose of selecting position for Foden Disinfector.	
27th December 1916.	Was visited by O.C. Sanitary Section 4th Division re. taking over the Vhulaten Gros area & inspected with him new several parts of the area	
28th December 1916 France 1/40000 ALBERT 57 & 62 d	Left CHIPILLY and arrived at Camp 14	
29 December 1916	Began a sanitary survey of district. Visiting BRAY in morning.	
30th November 1916	Visited Camp 20 in morning and camp 21 in afternoon	
31 November 1916.	Visited Headquarters Battalion in morning and walk round Suzanne in afternoon	

G. Chapman
Capt (Sanitary)
O.C. 83 Sanitary Section

83rd Sanitary Section

40 h.Pws

110/9143

COMMITTEE FOR THE
[ME]DICAL HISTORY OF THE WAR
Date 13 MAR. 1917

SECRET

Army Form C. 2118

WAR DIARY of 83rd SANITARY SECTION.
— or —
INTELLIGENCE SUMMARY. Vol 2. page 1.

(Erase heading not required.)

Instructions regarding War Diaries and Intelligence Summaries are contained in F.S. Regs., Part II. and the Staff Manual respectively. Title pages will be prepared in manuscript.

Hour, Date, Place	Summary of Events and Information	Remarks and references to Appendices
1st January 1917. Map Reference FRANCE 1/100,000 ALBERT. G.S.G.S. 2364. Sheet 13.	Visited Camps 20 & 21 to see progress of Sanitary arrangements.	
2nd Jany	Cpl REAVELL admitted to Hospital	
	Visited BRAY.	
3rd Jany	Visited Camp 21.	
4th Jany	Visited ANDOVER to see Sanitary arrangements	
5th Jany	Visited BRAY. "B.Echelon" Cpl. SILVER admitted to Hospital	
6th. Jany	Visited BRAY "B. Echelon"	
7th. Jany	Visited Camps 20-21	
8th Jany	Eleven N.C.O's men (from Regimental Sanitary Squads) reported for a weeks course of Sanitary Instruction.	
10th Jany	Two men from Regimental Sanitary Squads reported for a weeks course in Sanitary Instruction.	
11th. Jany.	Visited Camps 20 & 21 Two Privates (R.A.M.C.) Reinforcements reported for duty & taken on the strength accordingly.	
14th Jany	Visited MAUREPAS (B.16) to see water point	

SECRET.

of 63rd SANITARY SECTION

WAR DIARY

INTELLIGENCE SUMMARY. Vol 2. P.2.

Army Form C. 2118

Instructions regarding War Diaries and Intelligence Summaries are contained in F. S. Regs., Part II. and the Staff Manual respectively. Title pages will be prepared in manuscript.

(Erase heading not required.)

Hour, Date, Place	Summary of Events and Information	Remarks and references to Appendices
15th Jany.	Visited Camps 20 & 21. Thirteen N.C.O's men finished their course of Sanitary Instruction & returned to their units. Nine N.C.O's men from Regimental Sanitary Squads reported for a Weeks course of Sanitary Instruction.	
16th Jany	One man from Regimental Sanitary Squad reported for weeks course of Sanitary Instruction	
17th Jany	Visited Camp 23. One Private (RAMC) (Reinforcement) reported for duty & taken on the strength accordingly	
18th Jany	Visited Camps 20 & 21	
19th Jany	Visited BRAY to investigate case of Mumps	
20th Jany	Visited Camps 20 & 21.	
21st Jany	Visited MAUREPAS & Camp 23.	
22nd Jany.	Visited BRAY & "B" Echelon 10 N.C.O's men finished their course of Sanitary Instruction & returned to their units 11 N.C.O's men from Regimental Sanitary Squads reported for a Weeks course of Sanitary Instruction	
23rd Jany	1 Man from Regimental Sanitary Squad reported for a Weeks course of Sanitary Instruction.	

SECRET.

Instructions regarding War Diaries and Intelligence
Summaries are contained in F. S. Regs., Part II.
and the Staff Manual respectively. Title pages
will be prepared in manuscript.

WAR DIARY
or
INTELLIGENCE SUMMARY.

Army Form C. 2118

of 83rd Sanitary Section

Vol 8. p. 3.

(Erase heading not required.)

Hour, Date, Place	Summary of Events and Information	Remarks and references to Appendices
24th Jany.	Visited Camps 20 & 21. One inmate (Reinforcement) reported for duty & taken on the strength accordingly.	
26th Jany.	Visited BRAY & "B" Echelon.	
28th Jany. FRANCE 1/40,000 ALBERT. J.36. d.8.3.	Section G.Os. removed from Camp 19. to SAILLY LAURETTE. Map Ref. FRANCE. 1/40,000 ALBERT. J.36. d.8.3.	
29th Jany.	Commenced inspection of area. 10. N.C.Os. men of Regimental Sanitary Squads reported to their units having finished course of instruction in Sanitation. 4. N.C.Os. men of Regimental Sanitary Squads reported for Weeks course in Sanitation.	
30th Jany.	5 N.C.Os. men of Regimental Sanitary Squads reported for Weeks course in Sanitation. Selected sites for new latrines in SAILLY LAURETTE. Interviewed Area Commandant at CHIPILLY.	
31st Jany	Visited BEL AIR, to procure material for Workshop.	

G. Shand Capt.
R.A.M.C.(T)
O/C 83rd Sanitary Section

40/1991

40 Div.

83rd Sanitary Section

COMMITTEE FOR THE
MEDICAL HISTORY OF THE WAR
Date 4 APR. 1917

SECRET

Army Form C. 2118.

WAR DIARY
INTELLIGENCE SUMMARY. of 83rd SANITARY SECTION.
Vol X. page 1.

(Erase heading not required.)

Instructions regarding War Diaries and Intelligence Summaries are contained in F.S. Regs., Part II. and the Staff Manual respectively. Title pages will be prepared in manuscript.

Hour, Date, Place	Summary of Events and Information	Remarks and references to Appendices
1st Feby. 1917 For Reference FRANCE/W/100 ALBERT 936. d.8.3.	Visited Camps 12 & 13.	
2nd. Feby 1917	Visited Camps 12 & 13 & 25, to note any improvements that could be carried out	
3rd Feby 1917.	Visited CHIPILLY & saw area Commandant. Visited Camps 12 & 13	
4th Feby 1917.	Visited CORBIE and SAILLY-LE-SEC.	
5th Feby 1917.	9 N.C.O's & men reported from Regimental Sanitary Squads for Sanitary instruction. Visited Camps 12 & 13 & 25.	
6th Feby 1917.	Visited Camps 12, 13. Noted progress. Selected latrine sites	
7th Feby 1917.	Visited CORBIE	
8th Feby. 1917.	Visited Camps 12 & 15, also made inspection of Cavalry Lines &c	
9th Feby 1917.	Visited CORBIE and SAILLY-LE-SEC.	

SECRET

Army Form C. 2118

WAR DIARY
or
INTELLIGENCE SUMMARY.

Of 63rd Sanitary Section Vol IX page 2

(Erase heading not required.)

Instructions regarding War Diaries and Intelligence Summaries are contained in F.S. Regs., Part II. and the Staff Manual respectively. Title pages will be prepared in manuscript.

Hour, Date, Place	Summary of Events and Information	Remarks and references to Appendices
January 10th 1917.	9 N.C.Os men of Regimental Sanitary Squads, detailed to spend at work to their different units having completed course of instruction in Sanitation. Made an inspection of Camp 124. No 1055 a/Cpl MASKELL reported back from 119th Brigade H.Q. for duty. No 92 SMITH " " 72/st	
January 12th 1917.	Visited Camp 124. 3 men of Regimental Sanitary Squads, reported for Works course in Sanitation. Visited CHIPILLY & saw Area Commandant. Inspected Water points. No. 1103. a/Cpl ALDOUS, reported back from 180th Brigade H.Q. for duty. Interviewed Staff Captain 24th Brigade re obtaining fatigue men for SAILLY LAURETTE and Camp 124.	
January 13th 1917.	Visited CHIPILLY & inspected Camps 122 & 123 with Area Commandant. One man from Regimental Sanitary Squads reported for Weeks course in Sanitation.	
January 14th 1917.	Visited Camps 124 & 125, & interviewed medical officers of units. Visited CORBIE.	

SECRET

Army Form C. 2118.

WAR DIARY
INTELLIGENCE SUMMARY.
of 83rd SANITARY SECTION

Vol IX page 3

(Erase heading not required.)

Hour, Date, Place	Summary of Events and Information	Remarks and references to Appendices
January 15th 1917	Visited CORBIE, interviewed A.D.M.S. 8th Division	
January 16th 1917	Visited Camp. 124.	
January 17th 1917	Visited Camp 124. and noted improvements in progress	
January 18th 1917	Visited Camp 124. Visited Corbie.	
January 19th 1917	Visited Camp 124.	
January 20th 1917	Visited Camp 124.	
January 21st 1917	Inspected Sailly LAORETTE area.	
January 22nd 1917	Inspected SAILLY LAURETTE area.	
January 23rd 1917	Inspected Camp of 24 Squadron R.F.C. - K.21.a.	
January 24th 1917	Inspected Camp 125.	
January 25th 1917	Visited BELAIR. Inspected Camps 124 and 12.	
January 26th 1917	Inspected SAILLY LAURETTE area.	
January 27th 1917	Inspected SAILLY-LE-SEC.	
February 28th 1917	Inspected Camps 125. & 124.	

140/2087.

No. 83. Sanitary Section.

COMMITTEE FOR THE
MEDICAL HISTORY OF THE WAR
Date —6 JUN.1917

SECRET

Vol 3/0

Army Form C. 2118.

WAR DIARY

— of —

INTELLIGENCE SUMMARY. of 83rd SANITARY SECTION

(Erase heading not required.)   VOL: X page 1.

Instructions regarding War Diaries and Intelligence Summaries are contained in F. S. Regs., Part II. and the Staff Manual respectively. Title pages will be prepared in manuscript.

Hour, Date, Place	Summary of Events and Information	Remarks and references to Appendices
1st March, 1917. Map Reference FRANCE ALBERT 1/40,000 J 36 d 83.	Visited CHIPILLY and Camp 12.	
2nd March. 1917	Inspected CHIPILLY and Camp 12.	
3rd March. 1917.	Visited to SAILLY-LE-SEC.	
4th March. 1917.	Visited railhead at Corbie.	
5th March. 1917.	Conference at ETINEHEM. Visited Camp 124.	
6th March. 1917	Inspected Camp 124.	
7th March. 1917	Inspected CHIPILLY and Camp 12	
8th March. 1917	Visited SUZANNE and CORBIE RAILHEAD	
9th March. 1917. Map ALBERT G.8. d 13	Moved to SUZANNE and visited Camps 18 and 19	
10th March. 1917	Visited FRISE BEND, HEM and HEM WOOD and LINGER CAMPS.	

(73989) W4141—463. 400,000. 9/14. H.&J.Ltd. Forms/C. 2118/10.

WAR DIARY or INTELLIGENCE SUMMARY.

(Erase heading not required.)

Army Form C. 2118.

Hour, Date, Place	Summary of Events and Information	Remarks and references to Appendices
11th March, 1917	Visited HEM WOOD, HOWITZER WOOD, SUZANNE and Camp 17.	
12th March, 1917	Visited CLERY. Three R.A.M.C.T. Reinforcements reported at Chateau, SUZANNE.	
13th March, 1917	Visited P.C. WURZEL and P.C. VIOLETTE.	
14th March, 1917	Visited Camp 17 and FRISE BEND.	
15th March, 1917	Inspected Camps 18 and 19.	
16th March, 1917	Visited LINGER CAMPS.	
17th March, 1917	Visited Camp 17, HEM FARM and WATER POINTS.	
18th March, 1917	Visited CLERY, HALLE, PERONNE and ST REDEGONDE for water testing.	
19th March, 1917	Visited FRISE BEND.	
20th March, 1917	Inspected SUZANNE area.	

Army Form C. 2118.

WAR DIARY
or
INTELLIGENCE SUMMARY.
(Erase heading not required.)

Instructions regarding War Diaries and Intelligence Summaries are contained in F.S. Regs., Part II. and the Staff Manual respectively. Title pages will be prepared in manuscript.

Hour, Date, Place	Summary of Events and Information	Remarks and references to Appendices
21st March, 1917.	Visited Camps 18 and 19 and LINGER CAMPS.	
22nd March, 1917.	With D.A.D.M.S. visited CLERY and P.C. JEAN; later visited CLERY alone.	
23rd March, 1917.	Moved to P.C. JEAN with section.	
Sheet 62c. H1.point 2. 24th March, 1917.	Visited PC VIOLETTE and PC WURZEL.	
25th March, 1917.	Inspected CURLU.	
26th March, 1917.	Visited CLERY, HEM WOOD and LE FORÊT.	
27th March, 1917.	Inspected FARGNY VALLEY and LINGER CAMPS.	
28th March, 1917. H.Q.	Section moved into new billet.	
29th March, 1917.	Visited LA CRANNIERE.	
30th March, 1917.	Sick	
31st March, 1917.	Sick	

Robert Paton Jackson
Major
3rd Sanitary Section

(73989) W4141—463. 400,000. 9/14. H.&J.Ltd. Forms/C. 2118/10.

www.ingramcontent.com/pod-product-compliance
Lightning Source LLC
Chambersburg PA
CBHW081245170426
43191CB00037B/2049